Betty White.

Who Was
Betty White?

by Dana Meachen Rau

illustrated by Laurie A. Conley

Penguin Workshop

To all the talented, kind, charming,
and silly older women in my life—DMR

PENGUIN WORKSHOP
An imprint of Penguin Random House LLC, New York

First published in the United States of America by Penguin Workshop,
an imprint of Penguin Random House LLC, New York, 2023

Visit us online at penguinrandomhouse.com.

Library of Congress Control Number: 2023020561

Printed in the United States of America

ISBN 9780593659809 (paperback)   10 9 8 7 6 5 4 3 2 1 WOR
ISBN 9780593659816 (library binding)   10 9 8 7 6 5 4 3 2 1 WOR

Contents

Who Was Betty White?

On May 8, 2010, Betty White opened a backstage door and stepped onto the set of *Saturday Night Live*. This popular weekly show had been on television for thirty-five years.

It featured famous celebrities performing funny skits in front of a live studio audience. As Betty stood under the stage lights, the audience went wild. She smiled at their applause. At age eighty-eight, she was the oldest person to ever host the show.

She had plenty of experience in front of audiences. She had performed on radio, television, stage, and in the movies. She had been on game shows, variety shows, talk shows, comedies, dramas, and soap operas. She was even a television producer at a time when that was a very rare role for women.

During the opening of the show that night, Betty made jokes about her age, and she thanked her fans. Earlier in the year, many of them joined in on a social media campaign called "Betty White to Host SNL (please?)!" More than five hundred thousand people signed a petition to urge the producers to invite her onto the show. They listened and booked her for the Mother's Day episode, also inviting many other famous female comedians to perform in skits with her.

Wearing a sparkly outfit and her bright, beautiful smile, Betty said, "I feel so loved. Thank you." She was not only speaking to the audience in the studio but to everyone watching on television at home. She did not disappoint her fans. Her talent, charm, and silliness on *Saturday Night Live* won her an Emmy Award for Outstanding Guest Actress in a Comedy Series, which was just one of many Emmys she had won. And at eighty-eight, her career—which began in the 1940s—was still going strong. She continued performing for the rest of her life.

She didn't just work hard in show business. She also supported people of color, the LGBTQIA+ community, and people with disabilities. And she loved animals. She spent lots of time and money for their care and protection.

Betty spread kindness and laughter throughout her extraordinary life.

CHAPTER 1
Showbiz Fever

Betty White was born on January 17, 1922, in Oak Park, Illinois. When she was a toddler, she and her parents, Horace and Tess, moved to the Los Angeles area of California. The three of them had lots of fun together. They loved telling jokes and playing silly games. They also loved animals and had many pets. The family didn't have much money. Her father made radios and sold them. Sometimes, instead of money, he traded the radios for dogs! They had to build a kennel in the backyard to hold them all.

Vacations were Betty's favorite family time. Every summer, they headed to the High Sierra Mountains or Yellowstone National Park.

They rode horses into the wilderness and
camped for weeks. She was fascinated by all
animals, big and small, and decided to be a forest

ranger when she grew up. But, at the time, only men could become rangers.

In school, she wrote stories. She even wrote

a play and made herself the lead. She also had a small part in a radio program. Betty caught "showbiz fever!" When she graduated from Beverly Hills High School in 1939, she looked for a job in show business.

Since she was a good singer, Betty was invited to participate in a television experiment. The broadcast didn't travel very far, however. The camera and actors performed on the sixth floor of the building, and the broadcast only went down to the first. But she had danced and sang on screen. It was a historic moment—one of the first television broadcasts on the West Coast!

But Betty's career would have to wait. World War II changed her plans. For four years, she worked for the American Women's Voluntary Services, driving a supply truck to soldiers stationed in the hills of Hollywood and Santa Monica. She became close to one young man,

and they married before he went off to war. After two years, they decided to part ways.

When the war ended in 1945, she joined a nearby theater and performed in a few plays. There, she met a man named Lane Allan. He suggested that she audition for radio shows. At that time, people listened to all sorts of comedy, adventure, news, and drama shows on the radio. They didn't have televisions yet.

Every week, she went to radio stations asking if they had work for her. And every week she got the same answer—"Nothing today." But soon, she started getting small parts.

Betty also got the chance to act in the movie *The Daring Miss Jones*. It was filmed on location in the mountains. Besides acting, she also assisted the director with lots of little jobs, including handling two trained bear cubs. After six weeks of the fun and challenges of animals and acting, she was glad to get home.

Soon she and Lane got married. She moved into his apartment along with his wedding present to her—a puppy named Bandit.

After more auditions, Betty started getting more jobs—this time on television! Television was very new in the 1940s. Los Angeles only had a few stations, and very few people even owned televisions. After she appeared on some comedy and game shows, people started to notice her talent. Al Jarvis was a famous Los Angeles disc jockey on the radio. One day he called her and asked if she would be interested in joining him on his new television program *Hollywood on Television*. Betty said yes!

CHAPTER 2
Live on Television

Hollywood on Television first aired in 1949 from the small KLAC-TV station in Los Angeles. At age twenty-seven, Betty's official television career had begun. The show aired live, five days a week for five hours a day. Jarvis and Betty sat behind a desk. He played records, and then the two of them chatted between songs. Within the week, letters poured in from fans who said they liked the conversation more than the music. So in the second week, they got rid of the records and filled the five hours discussing both silly and serious topics, sometimes with the help of special guests. Betty delighted audiences so much that by the third week, the network added more time to the weekday shows and even added a show on Saturdays.

Betty didn't mind the hard work of filming a live broadcast every day. She liked not having a script, making up things on the spot, and meeting interesting people. She also liked performing commercials, usually about fifty in each show. Every day was a thrill—and a chance to make mistakes, too. Often, the cast had so much fun that they got the giggles.

The show had expanded to include a sports report, music, and other features. The network added an evening show to showcase new entertainers, and another show focused on Betty giving advice. Bandit even came along! After about two years, Al Jarvis moved on to a new job. In only a few months, Betty became the new host of *Hollywood on Television*.

Meanwhile, Betty's husband, Lane, wished she would work less and be home more. They divorced, and she moved back home with her parents, Bandit, her new dog Stormy, and her parents' dog, Dancer.

Betty was becoming famous! In 1953, she won an Emmy Award for her work on *Hollywood on Television*. These awards, which started in 1949, were given to actors, directors, writers, and other people who work in television in the Los Angeles area.

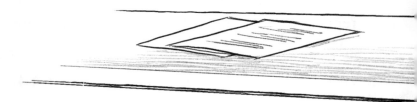

HOLLYWOOD
on
TELEVISION

With her career going so well, Betty and two of her coworkers started the production company Bandy Productions (named after her dog). Their first project was a new show called *Life with Elizabeth*, a comedy about Elizabeth, played by Betty, and her husband Alvin. The half-hour shows were filled with short scenes of the couple dealing with funny situations with titles like: *Late for a Party*, *Ping Pong*, and *Everything Goes Wrong*. She worked harder than she ever had before. She hosted *Hollywood on Television* all week and then rehearsed *Life with Elizabeth* on Friday nights. After Saturday's *Hollywood on Television* show, she fit in one more *Life with Elizabeth* rehearsal before performing the broadcast live at the Music Hall Theater in Beverly Hills on Saturday nights. Sunday was her only day off. But the hard work was worth it. Not only was she an entertaining actress, but she was *Life with Elizabeth*'s producer.

The director of the show, Betty Turbiville, was also a woman. Not many women held such important positions in Hollywood at the time.

Hollywood on Television and *Life with Elizabeth* ended, and a big national network had noticed Betty. The executives at NBC were charmed by her personality and wanted her to host her own variety show. Everything at a national network was new for her—hair, makeup, and wardrobe assistants, and her own dressing room! *The Betty White Show* would only be thirty minutes a day, much less than she was used to. It premiered all over the country in early 1954 and included guest interviews, performances by a band, comedy skits, children's segments, and animal features. Tap dancer Arthur Duncan became a cast member. Some stations in the southern United States told NBC that they would no longer broadcast *The Betty White Show*

if they didn't remove Arthur, because he was
Black. Betty was shocked and angry. She refused
to fire Arthur and said, "Live with it." She then
featured him on the show even more often.

   The Betty White Show lasted to the end of

Arthur Duncan on *The Betty White Show*

that year, and at the very beginning of the next, Betty hosted the 1955 Rose Parade on New Year's Day in Pasadena, California. She went on to host the parade for twenty more years.

Also in that year, she served as the Honorary Mayor of Hollywood. It was an unofficial position voted on by fans. Betty had grown up in Los Angeles and become a celebrity there. Soon the rising star would cross the United States to see what acting jobs New York City had to offer.

CHAPTER 3
Playing Games

Betty loved California, but New York was where most major television networks filmed their shows. In June of 1955, she appeared on the game show *What's My Line?* A panel of celebrity guests, like Betty, asked a contestant yes or no questions to guess their job. Game shows like this had become a huge hit with the growing popularity of television. Appearances on game shows became regular work for her. She had always loved puzzles and games. Her experience with live television, and her smart, friendly, and sweet personality were a perfect fit. During her career, she appeared on so many that she became known as the Queen of the Game Show.

One of the most popular game shows was *Password*. Celebrity and contestant pairs gave each other clues to guess words. The show premiered in the fall of 1961, and Betty was a guest its third week on air. Allen Ludden

was the host. Betty enjoyed Allen's sense of humor and how welcoming he was to all of his guests. When she was back home in California, she enjoyed watching *Password* on television.

The next year, Allen visited Los Angeles and took Betty to see a play. While they were chatting, she learned that his wife had died and that he had three children. That summer she and Allen were invited to perform in a play at small theaters in Massachusetts and Maine. She spent time enjoying the summer with Allen and his children, David, Martha, and Sarah.

Between acting jobs on the West Coast, Betty often visited New York as a game show guest, and also to see Allen. Before long, she realized she was in love. And so was he. One night while out to dinner, Allen gave her a diamond ring and asked her to marry him. But she didn't see how it could work. She loved California and didn't want to move to New York. Betty said no to Allen's proposal.

Allen wouldn't give up. He strung the engagement ring on a chain and wore it around his neck so she would see it every time they got together. Still, she said no. The next Easter, he sent her a stuffed rabbit wearing diamond earrings with a note that said "Please say YES." She finally agreed. The wedding was on June 14, 1963, the year Betty turned forty-one. The couple moved into a new home in Chappaqua, New York, where she, Allen, the children, and two poodle puppies made a new family. While Allen continued to host *Password*, show business kept Betty busy, too. She was still a guest on game shows, performed in summer plays, and started hosting the Macy's Thanksgiving Day Parade in New York City.

After *Password* ended in 1967, Betty and Allen moved to California. Betty was pleased to return to her home state. They formed a production company: Albets Enterprises, Inc. (combining their names Allen and Betty). Allen urged her to create a show around animals, since she loved them so much. In 1971, Albets

Enterprises, Inc., produced a show called *Pet Set*. During the half-hour episodes, Betty interviewed celebrities and their pets. She also invited exotic pet guests, such as Kojak the

miniature horse, Sultan the Bengal tiger, and Major the black-maned lion. The show was on once a week and ran for thirty-nine episodes.

Recognizing her devotion to animals, the

Morris Animal Foundation, a group that works for the health and protection of animals, invited Betty to be a trustee. A trustee helps make decisions for an organization. She was also asked to be a trustee for the Greater Los Angeles Zoo Association. Besides helping to raise money to support the care of the animals, she loved to visit the Los Angeles Zoo. Betty and an elephant named Gita often took early walks through the zoo before it opened on Saturday mornings.

CHAPTER 4
Comedic Characters

Betty didn't just like to be *on* television—she also liked to watch it, including a show starring one of her very best friends, Mary Tyler Moore. *The Mary Tyler Moore Show* was about a young woman living in the city of Minneapolis. Her character worked as an associate producer at a television station. Mary was also one of Betty's close friends.

Betty was thrilled when she was asked to play a guest character named Sue Ann Nivens on Mary's show. Sue Ann was a supersweet homemaker with a hidden mean streak. Betty had a great time playing that role. Her guest spot went so well that they wrote more scripts for her, and Sue Ann became a regular character for that season and the next three until the show ended. While on *The Mary Tyler Moore Show*, Betty won Emmy Awards for her outstanding performances two years in a row, 1975 and 1976. Emmys, which had only been regional Los Angeles awards when Betty won her first one more than twenty years before, now were given on the national level.

Betty had many friends in show business. Another good friend, the actress and comedian Carol Burnett, also had her own show. *The Carol Burnett Show* was a collection of funny skits—a perfect showcase for Betty. Johnny Carson, the host of *The Tonight Show* at that time, often invited Betty as a guest to perform in comedy scenes. In one, she and Johnny are pretending to have a romantic dinner on the beach when the high tide comes in—and 550 gallons of water crashed onto the stage, and on them! Betty was willing to do anything for a laugh!

Betty at the Emmy Awards ceremony in 1976

Life changed for Betty in 1981 when Allen died of cancer. She was devastated. They had been married for eighteen years. But she kept on working and finding ways to share laughter. On *Mama's Family*, a series about a grouchy woman based on one of the skits from *The Carol Burnett Show*, Betty played the role of Ellen, her spoiled, rich daughter. She also appeared as a guest on many game shows. In 1983, she became a game show host like Allen had been. She was so good at hosting *Just Men!* that she won another Emmy.

Two years later, when Betty was sixty-three years old, she joined the cast of a weekly show that became one of the most famous in television history. *The Golden Girls* was about four older women living together in Miami. She played a sweet character named Rose Nylund, who comes from the small town of St. Olaf, Minnesota. She and the cast read through the script on Mondays, rehearsed all week, and taped the show on Fridays. They did it all over again with a new script and a new story each week.

A show focusing on the lives of older women hadn't been done before, but the writers and creators were sure it would be a hit. In its first week, *The Golden Girls* was the number-one watched comedy show on television. Even though many of the jokes were about the day-to-day lives of older women, fans of all ages liked it. It appeared on top-ten lists for six of its seven seasons, had millions of viewers, and won lots of Emmy Awards. The show was so popular that they had a royal fan in London. They were invited for a special onstage performance for the mother of Queen Elizabeth II.

The Golden Girls

The Golden Girls was a half-hour situation comedy (sitcom) set in the city of Miami, Florida, that ran on television from 1985 to 1992. Betty White played Rose Nylund, who lived with three other women: Dorothy Zbornak and her mother Sophia Petrillo, played by actresses Bea Arthur and Estelle Getty, and Blanche Devereaux, played by Rue McClanahan. The four characters were all very different, which led to many misunderstandings and laughs. They sometimes disagreed, but always supported and loved one another. The women often talked about their lives around the kitchen table while eating cheesecake. And while the show was filled with funny scenes, it occasionally touched on serious topics, too, including discrimination against the LBGTQIA+ community and people of color, the environment, and politics.

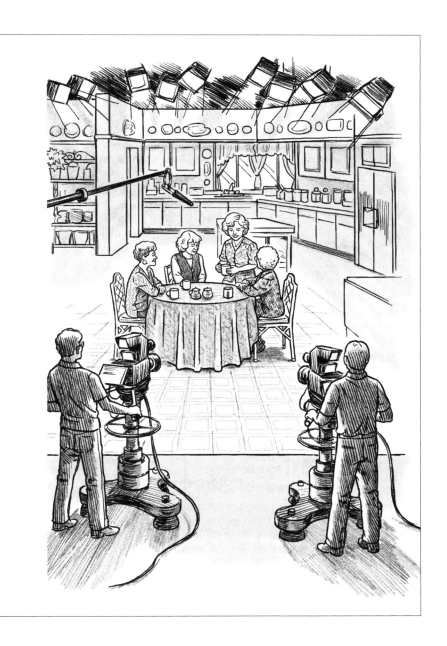

The show still has so many fans that in 2022, thousands attended Golden-Con, a convention in Chicago that included costume contests, trivia contests, and a dance party. That same year, a restaurant called Golden Girls Kitchen opened in Beverly Hills, California, serving plenty of cheesecake.

The Golden Girls is considered one of the best—and funniest—sitcoms of all time. And its theme song, "Thank You for Being a Friend," reached top spots on popular music charts.

CHAPTER 5
Celebrating Betty

When *The Golden Girls* ended in 1992, Betty was seventy years old. For the next two decades, she was busier than ever. She appeared in the movies, in comedies and dramas on television, and even on a soap opera. Over her career, she had done just about everything there was to do in show business. And her long career was often celebrated.

In 1995, she was accepted into the Television Academy Hall of Fame. In her speech, she said, "Nobody—nobody has ever had more fun in this world doing what they do for a living than I have in television." Then in 2010, she received the Lifetime Achievement Award from the Screen Actors Guild, one of the highest honors for actors. At the ceremony, she reminded audiences that she wasn't done yet. "I was only eighty-eight last Sunday so I've got lots more stuff to do!"

Outside of acting, Betty still spent time working with the Morris Animal Foundation and the Los Angeles Zoo. She also supported BraveHearts, an organization that encourages horse riding as therapy for children with autism and for wounded veterans. She worked with Seeing Eye, a group that trains guide dogs for blind people. "I can't imagine being without animals," she said. In fact, she also joked that she likes animals more than humans.

Koko was a three-hundred-pound western lowland gorilla who became one of the most special animals in Betty's life. Betty met her at the Gorilla Foundation preserve in the Santa Cruz Mountains in 2004. Koko was famous for her use of sign language. When Koko met Betty, she recognized her from watching *The Golden Girls* on television! Koko had a special name for Betty—the sign for *lipstick*.

In 2009, Betty appeared in the movie *The Proposal*, starring Ryan Reynolds and Sandra Bullock. As fussy, rude Grandma Annie, Betty once again showed her talent for being funny. Then in 2010, she appeared in a Super Bowl advertisement for the candy bar Snickers. In it, she trash-talks the other players in a rough game of football. Everyone thought she was hysterical! Older fans who had followed her long career and new ones alike wanted to see more of Betty! That year she became the oldest person to host *Saturday Night Live* at age eighty-eight, after fans created a petition on social media that hundreds of thousands of people signed.

That same year, a childhood dream of Betty's finally came true. The United States Forest Service sent her a letter declaring that she was now an honorary forest ranger! At a ceremony in Washington, DC, she received a certificate, badge, and forest ranger hat.

At the time, Betty said, "I know this is an honorary position, but it's also one where I can use a voice to try to protect the remaining beautiful parts of this gorgeous world we live on."

Also in 2010, she took on a new role in the sitcom *Hot in Cleveland* as the landlord named Elka Ostrovsky. At first, she said she would only do one episode. She and the other four actresses on the show had so much fun working together that Betty remained on the show for all six seasons. She won even more awards—including a Guinness World Record for the Longest Career for an Entertainer (female).

When *Hot in Cleveland* ended in 2015, Betty was ninety-three years old. But she still had more work to do! She voiced the animated characters of Grammy Norma in the movie *The Lorax*, Beatrice in *SpongeBob SquarePants*, and Bitey White in *Toy Story 4*.

Betty was going to turn one hundred years old on January 17, 2022. Big celebrations were being planned. But on New Year's Eve 2021, she passed away at her home in Los Angeles, California. Fans were sad, but still celebrated the

life of this amazing woman. They remembered her and her work in social media posts, news articles, and documentaries.

Betty White's career began when television began in the 1940s. She spent her long life working hard to spread joy, kindness, and laughter to all who watched.

Timeline of Betty White's Life

1922	Born January 17 in Oak Park, Illinois
1941–1945	Volunteers for the American Women's Voluntary Services during World War II
1949–1953	Appears on *Hollywood on Television*
1953	Wins regional Emmy Award for Most Outstanding Female Personality for *Hollywood on Television*
1953–1955	Produces and stars in *Life with Elizabeth*
1954	Hosts the national NBC show *The Betty White Show*
1973–1977	Plays Sue Ann Nivens on *The Mary Tyler Moore Show*
1975–1976	Wins Emmys for Outstanding Continuing Performance by a Supporting Actress in a Comedy Series
1985–1992	Plays Rose Nylund on *The Golden Girls*
1986	Wins Emmy for Outstanding Lead Actress in a Comedy Series
2010	Hosts *Saturday Night Live*
	Wins Emmy for Outstanding Guest Actress in a Comedy Series
	Becomes an honorary US forest ranger
2010–2015	Plays Elka Ostrovsky on *Hot in Cleveland*
2016	Voices Beatrice in episode of *SpongeBob SquarePants*
2019	Voices Bitey White in the movie *Toy Story 4*
2021	Dies at age ninety-nine on December 31 in Los Angeles

Timeline of the World

1925	Master jazz trumpeter Louis Armstrong begins his solo career as a musician and singer
1932	American aviator Amelia Earhart becomes the first woman to fly solo across the Atlantic Ocean
1939	Television is broadcast for the first time at the World's Fair in New York City by NBC
1947	Margaret Wise Brown's children's book *Goodnight Moon* is published
1952	Elizabeth II becomes the queen of England
1965	US Congress passes the Voting Rights Act to ensure fair elections for Black voters
1977	The first *Star Wars* movie, now called *Star Wars: A New Hope*, opens in theaters
1980	The colorful puzzle Rubik's Cube, invented by Hungarian designer Erno Rubik, is first sold in stores
1990	Paleontologist Sue Hendrickson discovers an almost complete *T. rex* skeleton in South Dakota
2005	YouTube launches its website, making video sharing possible across the world
2019	Gymnast Simone Biles wins her record-breaking twenty-fifth World Championship medal
2022	NASA's James Webb Space Telescope sends back the clearest images yet of our solar system and beyond

Bibliography

*Books for young readers

Boettcher, Steve, dir. *Betty White: First Lady of Television*.
Trinklein Productions, August 21, 2018. Peacock, 57 min.

*Bonsignore, Gregory. *That's Betty!: The Story of Betty White*.
Illustrated by Jennifer M. Potter. New York: Henry Holt and
Company, 2021.

Chang, Rachel. "Betty White's Love for Animals Began as a Child."
Biography.com, January 17, 2020. https://www.biography.
com/news/betty-white-animals-charity.

Gambino, Megan. "Betty White on Her Love for Animals."
Smithsonian Magazine, May 14, 2012. https://www.
smithsonianmag.com/science-nature/betty-white-on-her-
love-for-animals-92610121/.

Kline, Robert, dir. *Betty White: Champion for Animals*. Enduring
Freedom Productions, 2012. DVD, 1 hr., 29 min.

Lachman, Brad, dir. *Celebrating Betty White: America's Golden
Girl*. NBC.com, January 31, 2022. 45 min.

Murray, Michael. "Betty White: Facebook Phenomenon at 88." *ABC News*, February 17, 2010. https://abcnews.go.com/WN/betty-white-urged-facebook-group-375000-people-growing/story?id=9864078.

Richmond, Ray. *Betty White: 100 Remarkable Moments in an Extraordinary Life*. Bellevue, WA: becker&mayer!, 2021.

White, Betty. *Betty & Friends: My Life at the Zoo*. New York: G. P. Putnam's Sons, 2011.

White, Betty. *Here We Go Again: My Life in Television*. New York: Scribner, 1995.

White, Betty. *If You Ask Me (And of Course You Won't)*. New York: G. P. Putnam's Sons, 2011.

White, Betty. *In Person*. New York: Doubleday, 1987.